INTRODUCTION

Since the late 1990s, Africa has grown in strategic importance to the interests of the United States. According to the National Intelligence Council's *Global Trends: 2015,* twenty-five percent of North American oil imports are projected to come from West Africa by 2015.[1] Records indicate that in 2006, African crude oil accounted for 22% of U.S. imports of crude oil.[2] China is seen as a growing competitor for access to this oil and other natural resources throughout Africa. In terms of security, the United States is concerned with ungoverned spaces throughout the Maghreb and Sahel (see appendix A), where violent extremists are free to plan and conduct their activities. Somalia is in turmoil and risks being overtaken by Islamist insurgents. Human trafficking and the illicit trafficking of drugs and other contraband, piracy, poor governance, corruption, human rights violations, armed conflicts, desertification, and poverty present a complex set of challenges to the United States and international community. The recent regime changes in Tunisia and Egypt demonstrate just how dissatisfied Africans in the Maghreb are.

As U.S. military action wanes in Iraq and intensifies in Afghanistan, the last thing the United States wants is to have to deploy thousands of troops to remote regions of Africa and explain to the American public why their sons and daughters must spill their blood on foreign soil yet again. Even now, the current administration is hesitant to intervene militarily on behalf of opposition forces to Muammar Khadafi and his Libyan regime. Without the support of the international community and the United States, fledgling democracies incapable of or unwilling to address the stressors that lead to conflict risk becoming failed states. The United States does not want groups like Al Qaeda to thrive in ungoverned spaces, where they can plan, prepare for, coordinate, and initiate attacks against the United States. If such a scenario occurs in Africa, the United States may certainly be faced with a decision to send troops as it did in Afghanistan. After nearly a decade of war, U.S. strategy is relatively shifting from contingency planning (how to fight the next war) to strategic planning (how to avoid the next war). Of the five phases of joint campaigns or operations described in Joint Publication 3-0, Phase 0 (Shape) has become critically important to U.S. efforts in Africa. Iraq and Afghanistan have highlighted the U.S. military's prowess during Phase III (Dominate) operations and have exposed U.S. shortcomings during Phase IV (Stabilize). If executed properly, Phase 0 efforts in Africa can help reduce the stressors that lead to conflict and instability and can help assure access should a contingency arise.

These shaping efforts require a whole-of-government approach designed to wield all instruments of national power. The National Security Strategy 2010, states that

> The Administration will refocus its priorities on strategic interventions that can promote job creation and economic growth; combat corruption while strengthening good governance and accountability; responsibly improve the capacity of African security and rule of law sectors; and work through diplomatic dialogue to mitigate local and regional tensions before they become crises.[3]

The complexities of executing Phase 0 operations in Africa are numerous given the fact that multiple agencies are at work, theoretically trying to achieve the same end to

> enhance international legitimacy and gain multinational cooperation in support of defined military and national strategic objectives…shaping perceptions and influencing the behavior of both adversaries and allies, developing allied and friendly military capabilities for self-defense and coalition operations, improving information exchange and intelligence sharing, and providing U.S. forces with peacetime and contingency access.[4]

This paper examines Phase 0 activities in the Maghreb and Sahel, a region of Africa crucial to U.S. interests because of its potential and because of its volatility. Current Phase 0 efforts in the Maghreb and Sahel nations of Africa focus on counterterrorism, countering violent extremist ideology, building partner nation security capacity, good governance, and economic development, but lack appropriate interagency synchronization and are improperly balanced between the development approach and the defense approach. Programs are DoS-led, yet the State Department is forced to rely heavily on DoD for much of the funding, resources, and manpower needed to execute. The result is what is perceived to be the militarization of foreign policy. This paper will first explore the many problems and challenges of this region of the world, highlighting the importance of successful shaping operations in the Maghreb and Sahel. It will then discuss and analyze some of the Phase 0 efforts currently underway. The conclusion will include recommendations designed to address potential gaps in U.S. shaping efforts across the Maghreb and Sahel. It is absolutely critical that the United States gets this right. Failure to do so could mean sending off the next generation of Americans to fight in a war that could have been prevented.

CHALLENGES OF THE MAGHREB & SAHEL REGION OF AFRICA

The recent toppling of Tunisia's former president of 23 years, Zine El Abidine Ben Ali, on January 14, 2011, followed by former Egyptian President Hosni Mubarek's resignation on February 12, 2011, illustrates perfectly a common sentiment among the people of North and West Africa, that of dissatisfaction with corrupt and ineffectual government. While democracy is spreading in Africa, the democracy brand is being tainted by the practice of authoritarian democracy, whereby corrupt leaders ensure their own election or attempt to change the rules of tenure entirely to secure their position of power and wealth. This past decade alone, between 2000 and 2011, Guinea-Bissau, Mauritania, Togo, Niger, and Tunisia have experienced regime changes precipitated by coups d'état. Mauritania experienced two coups. Current Mauritanian President Mohamed Ould Abdel Aziz helped instigate the 2005 coup and led the 2008 coup against the unpopular Sidi Ould Cheikh Abdallahi. The common thread for all of these regime changes was poor governance by corrupt leaders. A few elites would get rich, while most of the population would continue to suffer from poverty. In fact, countries like Liberia, Niger, Sierra Leone, Togo, Guinea, Guinea-Bissau, Burkina Faso, and Mali rank among the poorest countries in the world.

Where poor governance and poverty exist, it is not surprising to discover a lack of education or professionalization of armed forces and/or law enforcement. Human trafficking becomes a lucrative prospect for some. Piracy in the Gulf of Guinea proves profitable for others. Crime becomes attractive to the have-nots, and recruitment of disillusioned youth by violent extremists becomes easier. Even in Tunisia, though the primary grievances were economic in nature, Muslim extremists attempted to seize the opportunity to call for an Islamic state and an all-out rejection of democracy. The world waits to see who will replace Mubarek in Egypt and keeps a watchful eye on the Muslim Brotherhood, an Islamic movement and political group with a controversial history and a specific Islamic agenda.[5]

Just how serious is the terrorist threat in North Africa to U.S. interests? Al Qaeda in the Islamic Maghreb (AQIM) is a relatively new franchise of Al Qaeda. Upon declaring allegiance to Usama bin Laden in September 2006, the *Groupe Salafiste pour la Prédication et le Combat*, or Salafist Group for Preaching and Combat (GSPC), changed its name in January 2007 to AQIM. The GSPC was founded in 1998 with the goal of instituting an Islamic state in place of the Algerian government.[6] Terrorist activities were initially limited to within Algeria, but over time Algerian security services severely hampered the GSPC's ability to operate exclusively in Algeria. Consequently, current AQIM activities have shifted towards the Sahel into countries like Mali and Mauritania. Porous borders and ungoverned spaces have allowed AQIM to regroup, refit, recruit, and train relatively unmolested by national authorities.

Kidnap for ransom, smuggling, and extortion appear to be the major funding source for AQIM. Attacks are in the form of ambushes, roadblocks, and bombings. Recent notable acts of terror by AQIM include a failed suicide bomb attack against the French embassy in Nouakchott, Mauritania preceded by the June 2009 killing of American Christopher Leggett also in Nouakchott, Mauritania;[7] the June 2009 assassination of a high-ranking Malian army officer at his home in Timbuktu, Mali;[8] the May 2009 execution of British hostage Edwin Dyer, kidnapped in Mali;[9] and the September 2008 beheading of a dozen Mauritanian soldiers after a coordinated ambush.[10] While AQIM appears to be a transnational threat, some suggest that "AQIM's overarching goal – the overthrow of the Algerian state – has not changed since the merger with al-Qa'ida…"[11] Countries that are willing to pay ransoms to AQIM in exchange for hostages are basically funding AQIM's ability to wage local jihad against the regimes they have been fighting for years.

To be sure, GSPC's merger with Al Qaeda has resulted in a broader scale of terror, but this is likely due to AQIM's attempts to maintain its association with and support from Al Qaeda. The number of actual adherents to Salafism within AQIM is unknown, but it is widely accepted that most Muslims throughout the Maghreb and Sahel subscribe to a moderate form of Islam and are not in support of the ideals espoused by AQIM.[12] This is not to say that the United States and international community should take AQIM lightly. AQIM is certainly a threat to

Algeria and over time has made enemies of Mali and Mauritania. Stability in these countries and throughout the region is degraded because of their terrorist activities. If left unchecked, their extreme ideology can and will permeate the minds of the discontent. What must be considered, however, is the true nature of the problem. While AQIM is clearly a force to be reckoned with, perhaps it is largely a symptom of a larger problem or set of problems.[13]

AQIM is not the only disenfranchised group in the region. The nomadic Tuareg have felt oppressed since the early 1900s, first with the French colonialists and subsequently with the governments of Mali and Niger.[14] Spread throughout the Sahara in Mali, Algeria, Libya, Niger, and Burkina Faso, this discontent group of people has taken up arms against authoritarian regimes of Mali and Niger throughout the past century. Desertification, drought, famine, ethnic division, weak and authoritarian governments, and infringement upon tribal lands all had a hand in the marginalization of the Tuareg. As the United States partners with the governments of Mali and Niger in the war on terror, the challenges for the United States become increasingly complex when factoring in the Tuareg. This is a local grievance that the United States does not want to get in the middle of, yet by sharing intelligence and by training and equipping the Malian and Nigerien militaries to fight AQIM, the United States has empowered these governments to more effectively fight against all enemies, foreign and domestic.[15] This could eventually lead to further alienating the Tuareg and possibly to the collaboration of, if not partnering of the Tuareg and AQIM.

Perhaps an even larger threat to stability in West Africa is the growing drug trade. According to a Congressional Research Service report on illegal drug trade in Africa

> On December 18, 2009, the U.S. Drug Enforcement Administration (DEA) announced the extradition from Ghana and arrest of three West Africans on narco-terrorism charges. The indictees allegedly agreed to transport cocaine for the

Colombian drug trafficking and terrorist organization, the Revolutionary Armed Forces of Colombia (FARC), from West Africa to Europe with the assistance and protection of regional affiliates of the Al Qaeda terrorist group.[16]

The report goes on to discuss the rapid rate at which cocaine has been rerouted from South America to various countries in West Africa, with Europe as the final destination. Actual use of cocaine is relatively low amongst Africans. Cannabis production, however, is significant "between an estimated 22% and 26% of global cannabis production."[17] and cannabis use among Africans is among the highest in the world. Criminal violence in the region is on the rise, as well as corruption among government and law-enforcement officials. When impoverished youth see drug lords driving around in their fancy cars, accompanied by pretty women, they begin to reconsider their options. Guinea-Bissau risks being dubbed Africa's first narco-state.[18] This could devolve into a repeat of Colombia where the Marxist-Leninist terrorist organizations the *Fuerzas Armadas Revolucionarias de* Colombia, or the Revolutionary Armed Forces of Colombia (FARC) used drug trafficking to finance their operations. Should a West African franchise of Al Qaeda, or any other terrorist organization with local grievances and/or global intentions, decide to fund their operations with drug money,[19] the United States and international partners could find themselves facing a formidable enemy with the capital to recruit, arm, train, and execute operations against U.S. interests in the region and on a global scale. Heightened instability in the Gulf of Guinea would limit legal trade and access to oil, disrupting regional and global economies.

To round out the list of challenges faced by the United States in Africa, China has proven to be a large competitor for natural resources on the continent. In the journal *International Affairs*, Professor of International Relations, Dr. Yahia H. Zoubir, goes so far as to suggest that Africa Command (AFRICOM) is producing African surrogates to possibly fight a proxy war with China.[20] He argues that the United States is providing security assistance to African nations rich in natural resources in order to avoid future direct military confrontation with terrorists and China. U.S. trained and financed regimes would essentially help the United States achieve its national objectives in the region, not unlike the Soviet Union's role in the Korean War where the Soviets aided the North Koreans but did not directly enter the war. While the United States would like to avoid a war in Africa and is certainly endeavoring to build partner nation capacity, these efforts are likely designed to defeat Islamic extremism and other sources of instability vice a military peer like China. Nevertheless, China has revealed itself to be the 800-pound gorilla on the continent and will have to be treated as either a competitor or a partner. What is at stake for the United States is influence in the region, competitiveness in trade with African countries, the advancement of human rights and shared values, and national security. China's "no-strings-attached" aid policy, whereby it provides aid to African nations regardless of its human rights record and internal governance, undermines U.S. and international efforts to bring about positive change.[21] While lucrative for China and for aid recipients like Sudan and Nigeria, such a policy is shortsighted and disruptive of U.S. long-term efforts to promote good governance and address stressors that lead to instability and ultimately threaten national security.

The Maghreb and Sahel's issues are numerous and present myriad challenges to U.S. interests in the region. Poor governance, corruption, unsecure spaces, poverty, trafficking of humans, the growing illicit drug trade, AQIM, ethnic strife, and China's growing influence all contribute to growing regional instability and now have the full attention of policy makers in the United States.

DISCUSSION AND ANALYSIS OF CURRENT PHASE 0 EFFORTS

What follows is an examination of current Phase 0 efforts in the Maghreb and Sahel. This section will discuss and analyze aspects of U.S. Africa Command (AFRICOM), the regional and country interagency apparatus, the Trans-Sahara Counter Terrorism Partnership (TSCTP), DoS and USAID capacity to shape the environment, and DoD efforts to bridge the capacity gap. This is not meant to be a comprehensive description of each of the programs currently underway. Such a description would be exhaustive and beyond the scope of this paper.

One major step the United States took in addressing the vast and complex challenges of Africa was the creation of U.S. Africa Command (AFRICOM). The Bush administration announced its creation on February 6, 2007. Prior to its establishment, efforts in Africa had been divided amongst three separate unified commands: "EUCOM, based in Germany, had 42 African countries in its AOR; CENTCOM, based in Florida, covered eight countries in East Africa, including those that make up the Horn of Africa; and PACOM, based in Hawaii, was responsible for the islands of Comoros, Madagascar, and Mauritius."[22] A Congressional Research Service report on AFRICOM describes the command's role, "AFRICOM's commander, General Kip Ward, views the Department of Defense's role in Africa as part of a 'three-pronged' U.S. government approach, with DOD, through AFRICOM, taking the lead on security issues, but playing a *supporting* role to the Department of State, which conducts diplomacy, and the United States Agency for International Development (USAID), which implements development programs."[23] AFRICOM's whole-of-government approach is relatively unique for a combatant command, but so is its mission. Interagency coordination is the mantra; in fact, the command has incorporated a significant non-DoD civilian staff, to include the unprecedented position of Deputy to the Commander for Civil-Military Activities (DCMA),[24] currently filled by Ambassador J. Anthony Holmes.

The Bush administration's announcement of the creation of AFRICOM sent shockwaves throughout the continent. U.S. combatant commands are generally associated with combat, and the notion that such a command was coming to Africa gave many on the continent pause, given the context of publicized U.S. offensive military interventions in Libya, Somalia, and Sudan, along with other U.S. military activity throughout the continent. Concerns over AFRICOM's intent ran rampant among the nations of Africa, and it took awhile for the command and U.S. government to recover from this strategic communication misstep.[25]

While AFRICOM has garnered much attention, it is just part of the overall U.S. effort in the region. Interagency coordination on African affairs begins in Washington, D.C. with various bureaus, offices, and liaison units. Within each country, the U.S. ambassadors lead the interagency effort. The Senior Defense Officials and/or Defense Attachés (SDO/DATT) are the military liaisons to the embassies. Some embassies may have an Office of Security Cooperation (OSC), led by a military official responsible for coordinating security assistance activities with the Partner Nation (PN).[26] According to USAID's website, "USAID currently has 23 bilateral field missions and three regional missions in sub-Saharan Africa."[27] Six of the bilateral field missions are in the Sahel region. These missions work closely with the U.S. embassies to achieve their development goals in country.

To ensure regional issues are addressed, a Regional Strategic Initiatives (RSI) group for the Trans-Sahara, chaired by ambassadors of the region, makes threat assessments, devises strategies, and develops plans and programs to address the threats.[28] Recently developed by the DoS' Office of the Coordinator for Counterterrorism (S/CT), this program ensures Country

Teams, while focused on their own country, understand the strategic situation in a regional context. Likewise, USAID has a West Africa Regional program designed to address challenges that go beyond country borders.[29]

Looking at the regional level, the RSI was a logical and needed step forward in gaining a regional perspective of the issues from the Country Teams and developing synergistic solutions involving all of the instruments of national power. Compared to the military system, though, this initiative seems like little more than a nice gesture. At the combatant command level, each Geographic Combatant Commander (GCC) fights for the resources and whatever else he needs in order to address the challenges of his assigned geographic area of responsibility (AOR). Vested with authority to command and make decisions, he takes ownership of that region of the globe and pushes his agenda aggressively.

The RSI is supposed to meet twice a year. According to the DoS' African Bureau, it has been an entire year since the RSI has met. The ambassadors also do not answer to a regional manager; they each answer directly to the President of the United States.[30] One report states that "the persistent structural misalignment between Combatant Commands, which take a regional approach to CT (and other security) challenges, and the State Department, which takes a bilateral approach based on U.S. country teams, complicates policy coherence."[31]

AFRICOM's Joint Interagency Coordination Group (JIACG) is another way to coordinate with all the other governmental agencies (OGAs) at the GCC level, but in the end it is a coordination tool;[32] and that is the inherent challenge of the interagency. No one really seems to be in charge. Meanwhile, DoD aggressively pushes forward with its shaping efforts, telling everyone else to lead, follow, or get out of the way; and in the opinion of one author, "Americans should understand the consequences of substituting generals and Green Berets for diplomats, and nineteen-year-old paratroopers for police and aid workers on nation-building missions."[33] Dr. Zoubir echoes the same sentiment by asking "What can special forces do against poverty, disease, corruption, lack of education, antidemocratic rule and rulers, and extremism in this impoverished region?"[34]

One specific U.S. government program designed to address the challenges of the Maghreb and Sahel is the Trans-Sahara Counter Terrorism Partnership (TSCTP). It is directed at transnational and extremists threats and is described as follows in AFRICOM's 2010 Posture Statement: "Special Operations Command, Africa (SOCAFRICA) conducts OEF-TS [Operation Enduring Freedom-Trans-Sahara] to counter the terrorism threat in North and West Africa. OEF-TS supports the DOS-led Trans-Sahara Counter Terrorism Partnership (TSCTP) by increasing our partners' capabilities to deny safe havens to terrorists, improving border security, promoting democratic governance, and reinforcing regional as well as bilateral military ties. OEF-TS activities are designed to defeat violent extremist organizations throughout the region."[35] The ten participating countries are Algeria, Burkina Faso, Chad, Mali, Mauritania, Morocco, Niger, Nigeria, Senegal, and Tunisia. The State Department leads the entire effort and focuses its department's efforts on diplomacy and good governance. USAID's efforts concentrate on development in areas such as education, youth empowerment, media, and good governance. DoD focuses on training, advising, and assisting the PN and building capacity.

There is a debate as to how serious a threat AQIM truly is to the United States. Dr. David Gutelius testified before the Senate Committee on Foreign Relations that "From a local perspective, neither GSPC nor AQIM have ever been considered major threats, nor has Salafism's more violent strain, per se. U.S. policy, on the contrary, has made these a priority and in so doing, has sometimes made worse local political and social dynamics in Sahel..."[36] He argues that the "The most critical regional issues are 1) environmental change 2) differential access to resources and extreme poverty 3) the growth of the value and volume in real terms of smuggling 4) and continued political disenfranchisement of northern populations..."[37] Considering TSCTP evolved out of the 2002 DoS Pan-Sahel Initiative (PSI) as a result of 9/11, one could argue that U.S. policy-makers failed to properly frame the problem in the Maghreb and Sahel. While building partner capacity is a good thing, the focus of the program and its follow-on program was and still is on AQIM. On the surface, this makes sense to Americans, especially in 2002 right after 9/11. The United States applied an American solution to an American problem - transnational terrorism bent on hurting the United States. TSCTP attempts to address issues such as promotion of good governance, anti-corruption, economic growth, education, and promotion of non-violence, but the military's OEF-TS component of TSCTP continues to be the most robust component of the program in spite of corrections over the last couple of years.[38] Intelligence capacity building and sharing, and the creation, training, and equipping of national CT units are great; but these programs focus on one thing: finding and killing terrorists. If more effort were applied towards development and good governance, then arguably there would be less terrorists to have to find and kill.

One reason that one might perceive the militarization of foreign policy is that, while DoS is tasked to be the lead in the interagency effort for reconstruction and stabilization, along with the development of strategies related to prevention and partner capacity building, per NSPD-44, *Management of Interagency Efforts Concerning Reconstruction and Stabilization*,[39] it lacks the man-power, resources, and funding enjoyed by DoD to execute. One of the contributors to *Short of General War: Perspectives on the Use of Military Power in the 21st Century* suggests that "The GCC's rise in preeminence reflects not only the void left by a weakened DoS, it also reflects a trend in the USG of increasing dependency on the military to carry out foreign affairs in recent decades."[40] In discussing theater strategy and regional security issues, Lieutenant Colonel Clarence J. Bouchat further highlights the imbalance between DoS and DoD by pointing out that "The DoS, for instance, has fewer than a brigade's worth of Foreign Service Officers (4,000-5,000 people) in the field. Their resources for tangible engagement activities also do not match the opportunities that DoD's schools, visits, exercises, equipment, and other cooperation activities offer."[41] Even Secretary of Defense, Robert M. Gates, noted in a 2007 speech "that the total foreign affairs budget for the DoS was less than what the DoD spends on health care coverage alone, and that the entire number of foreign officers equals the crew size of one aircraft carrier."[42] The African Bureau also acknowledges that human resourcing for DoS and USAID positions is one of their biggest issues.[43] For FY 2012, DoS plans on creating 184 new State Department positions.[44] USAID plans on creating 165 new positions.[45] This will help, but by no means does it demonstrate that growing the Foreign Service Officer corps is a priority.

It comes as no surprise then that the U.S. military has its fingerprints all over U.S. foreign policy initiatives, even in the areas of diplomacy and development. Given their deep pockets, planning abilities, training, manpower, equipment, unique skill sets, adaptability, and mission-first attitude, U.S. military personnel have taken the ball and have run with it. Members of DoD often find themselves executing DoS initiatives such as orchestrating education in democracy, good governance, and counter-violence ideology. Military Information Support Teams (MIST) become tools of the embassy as do Civil-Military Support Elements (CMSE), which help USAID (assuming they have a presence in country) execute their development programs. This is textbook application of interagency cooperation at the Country Team level; however, embassies can leverage these military entities only so far. Many MISTs are trained and focused at the tactical level. CMSEs can help get a well dug or build a school, but they are not trained in macroeconomic development. Macroeconomic experts are needed to coordinate, de-conflict, and synchronize development projects and to focus on large-scale development.

Meanwhile, some observers note insufficient synchronization of interagency efforts and a lack of requisite leadership from the State Department to coordinate the 3D (diplomacy, development, and defense) engagement concept. In discussing the militarization of U.S. foreign policy, Dennis R. Penn highlights what he perceives to be four impediments to this 3D concept. First, DoS and DoD look at the world differently. They do not even define regions of the world the same way, which impacts coordination and policy-making. Second, there is no senior non-DoD lead to oversee efforts in each region, resulting in differing views of purpose, lack of unity of effort, and overall synergy. Third, besides the combatant commands, there is no infrastructure to facilitate 3D engagement efforts. Finally, DoS and USAID lack resources to implement diplomacy and development initiatives.[46]

The current reality is that DoD has and will continue to shoulder much of the burden associated with achieving U.S. foreign policy objectives. A Huffington Post article disclosed piercing remarks made by Ambassador Ronald E. Neumann to the World Affairs Council at the University of Washington. The article stated that

> Even more disconcerting is the rising percentage of work within the development domain now being carried out by the U.S. military. Neumann highlighted how in 2002 94% of development-related activities were executed by State and USAID personnel, which only seems logical. However, by 2008 the military was doing 52% of the development work and this ratio has steadily grown more lopsided.[47]

Until the DoS receives the man-power, resources, and funding to take on more of a role in the diplomacy and development aspects of security cooperation, Soldiers, Sailors, Airmen, and

Marines will continue to attempt to fill in the gaps and will continue to take their leading role in enhancing the military capabilities of PNs. With this in mind, it is important to examine whether or not DoD is taking appropriate measures to meet the challenges of today and tomorrow. In order to properly address those challenges, there must be agreement as to what those challenges are and are likely to be. The 2002 National Security Strategy seems to have defined what the real threat is, "America is now threatened less by conquering states than we are by failing ones. We are menaced less by fleets and armies than by catastrophic technologies in the hands of the embittered few."[48] Nine years later in 2011 it is not readily evident how DoD has evolved to meet this asymmetric threat. DoD needs to figure out how to focus its efforts and resources on regional stabilization, the prevention of failed states, and the irregular threat of non-state actors, while at the same time ensuring that it can face a near-peer threat like China.

While DoS and USAID focus on diplomacy and development, DoD needs to adapt in order to be better equipped to professionalize the militaries of the Maghreb and Sahel. Tasked with taking the lead on the GWOT, USSOCOM has assigned many of its Special Operations Forces (SOF) to Foreign Internal Defense (FID) engagements across the globe. This FID mission has traditionally been associated with U.S. Army Special Forces (SF), but as stated in FM 3-24, "While FID has been traditionally the primary responsibility of the special operations forces (SOF), training foreign forces is now a core competency of regular and reserve units of all Services."[49] There simply is not enough SOF to cover down on global FID in the midst of war in two theaters. Additionally, the SOF engagements are typically with PN counterterrorism units or other SOF-like units and do not include ministerial-level (U.S. DoD equivalent) engagement, leaving conventional General Purpose Forces (GPF) to pair up with PN GPF forces. Iraq and Afghanistan have seen the rise of Military Transition Teams (MTTs), Embedded Training Teams

(ETTs), and other variants. The Army has also developed a concept for a modular brigade augmented for Security Force Assistance (SFA) and now has a SFA manual, FM 3-07.1. These are great solutions for Iraq and Afghanistan, but not necessarily for the rest of the world. A Brigade Combat Team (BCT) might not be a viable solution for SFA needs in some countries of the Maghreb or Sahel. Getting a small SOF team into some of these countries can be challenging at times, let alone trying to get buy-in from a HN or Country Team for an entire BCT. Unlike in Iraq or Afghanistan, the United States cannot just drop a BCT in the middle of a sovereign nation whenever it wants to. HN political constraints or other factors will determine the acceptable U.S. footprint. MTTs and ETTs are tailored specifically for Iraq and Afghanistan and are not being applied globally. What we have are short-term solutions for short-term problems. Iraq and Afghanistan will eventually end. What we will be left with are emerging threats coming out of unstable regions of the world lacking democratic institutions and professionalized security apparatus.

CONCLUSIONS AND RECOMMENDATIONS

In this age of globalization, where nations and regions of the world are becoming increasingly reliant upon each other, it is critical that the United States does what it can to assist partner nations and prevent regional destabilization. Each nation and region of the world needs something from the United States and has something to offer in return. Africa is no exception, specifically the countries of the Maghreb and Sahel. The challenges associated with these nations are many, and the United States has made great strides in addressing those challenges; but in order to bring stability to this complex and varied region, some fundamental changes must be adopted in how we approach the emerging threats of the future.

First, policy-makers must agree that the likely threat of tomorrow will be asymmetric in nature against non-state actors or individuals. While conflict with a nation-state like China, Iran, or North Korea is possible, it is more likely in the coming years that the United States will be forced to struggle with non-state belligerents using non-traditional means to gain credibility and legitimacy among the populace and achieve their ultimate end state. Conceptually, we need to be able to do both. Financially, we are limited in what we can do. The United States does not have an unlimited supply of money with which to build and maintain ships, submarines, jets, bombers, helicopters, and missiles. In fact, several projects have recently been terminated or temporarily suspended because of budget cuts. Several infantry battalions that were stood up in recent years will be stood back down. These fiscally challenging times have forced the United States to re-examine its priorities.

If the DoS continues to be responsible for leading the interagency effort, then it needs to be properly weighted to do so. Counter terrorism and counter insurgency expert, Dr. David Kilcullen, in his article titled "New Paradigms for 21st Century Conflict," points out that DoD is roughly 210 times larger than DoS and USAID combined and accounts for nearly half of defense spending worldwide. He puts forth "Our present spending and effort are predominantly military; by contrast, a 'global counterinsurgency' approach would suggest that about 80 percent of effort should go toward political, diplomatic, development, intelligence, and informational activity, and about 20 percent to military activity."[50] That may or may not be the right balance in terms of manning, funding, and/or resourcing, but what is clear is there needs to be a shift in balance that enhances non-military capacity. A strong military needs to be complemented by a strong law-enforcement arm. Law-enforcement needs to be backed up by a viable judicial system. That judicial system must be complemented by legislators and leaders who can govern diligently. Those governed must feel protected by their government and must know that their leaders are actively trying to solve issues like desertification, poverty, unemployment, social inequalities, and so on. By adapting to this new environment and by reallocating resources among the instruments of national power, the United States will be better suited to pursue its foreign policy objectives.

The 2010 Quadrennial Diplomacy and Development Review (QDDR), which was fashioned after DoD's Quadrennial Defense Review (QDR), has allowed DoS and USAID to conduct an internal review and map out a way forward as both organizations attempt to answer the question "How can we do better?"[51] This is a good tool and can be used to justify budget requests, while it helps to eliminate inefficiencies; but until DoS and USAID get significant plus ups, both organizations will be forced to lean on DoD for support.

Second, DoD must also come to terms with this new environment and adapt accordingly. Fiscal constraints, as evidenced by Secretary of Defense Gates' January 2011 announcement of billions of dollars of DoD budget cuts, are just another reminder of the heavy costs associated with Phase III and beyond operations. It is far less costly in blood and treasure to invest in Phase 0 "Shaping" operations. DoD must reevaluate its doctrine, organization, training, materiel, leadership, personnel, and facilities (DOTMLPF) in order to be relevant in the long war. While the threat of a conventional fight is out there, and while the United States must be prepared to counter such a threat, DoD must make the hard call and adapt to the current realities and likely threat of the future. DoD needs to institutionalize the recruitment, training, organization, and doctrine of U.S. GPF advisors and get away from the ad hoc solutions derived during times of conflict.

The Marine Corps is adopting this mindset and is beginning to make strides in this direction. *Send in the Marines: A Marine Corps Operational Employment Concept to Meet an Uncertain Environment* lays out initiatives currently underway such as the Security Cooperation Marine Air-Ground Task Force (SC MAGTF) – now labeled "Special Purpose MAGTF-(Security Cooperation)" (SPMAGTF-[Security Cooperation]) - and the Marine Corps Training and Advisor Group (MCTAG). The Center for Advanced Operational Culture Learning (CAOCL) and the Security Cooperation Education and Training Center (SCETC) were stood up to support these initiatives.[52] The decision to shrink the Marine Corps active duty ranks by 15,000 to 20,000 starting in 2015, revealed in Defense Secretary Gates' January 2011 budget cut announcement, will no doubt impact decisions made with regard to SPMAGTFs-(Security Cooperation). Planning and integrating SPMAGTFs (Security Cooperation) with scheduled Marine Expeditionary Unit (MEU) deployment cycles post-Iraq and Afghanistan with reduced manpower will require great thought and problem solving.

While the Marine Corps fleshes out these concepts, the Army needs to follow suit and develop a way forward for their service to meet the challenges of tomorrow. "Full spectrum" BCTs as described in the SFA manual, FM 3-07.1 are not the right answer. These Advise and Assist Brigades (AABs) were envisioned for Iraq[53] and are now being applied to Afghanistan. A step in the right direction would be an entire BCT's worth of soldiers devoted to recruiting, training, and organizing for scalable size elements to deploy and conduct SFA from the tactical level to the ministerial level. These soldiers would be the resident experts in advising PN forces, and during times of conflict could help surge the advisory capacity within the U.S. Army if needed. In 2007, the president of Center for a New American Security (CNAS), John Nagl, suggested the establishment of an Advisor Corps within the Army.[54] He acknowledges that his proposal would mean four fewer BCTs but argues that future challenges will require a robust advisory capability that is not ad hoc. Trained advisors are individuals who already know how to shoot, move, and communicate; and while these are perishable skills, it is also accepted that the best way to learn is to teach. Full time teachers, trainers, and advisors will require training and education in language, culture, negotiations, instructing, and advising. A full spectrum approach to advising will require emphasis on war fighting, while it concurrently attempts to impart advisory skills and training. Determining the right balance between a DoD, which is trained and equipped to fight a military peer and a DoD, which can address the likely challenges of an asymmetric environment is important, and it begins with the realization that change is needed.

Lastly, the United States needs to do a better job of shaping perceptions of U.S. actions and intentions. One way to do this is to get other stakeholders involved. The United States needs to partner with European countries affected by the flow of drugs and other contraband coming from West Africa and ensure they are doing their part to stem the flow. The United States needs to encourage their investment in countering this growing problem, as it threatens stability in the region, contributes to the growing drug problem in Europe, and ultimately contributes to lessened global serenity. The United States must carefully evaluate how to proceed with China on the African continent. An open dialogue must exist, where the United States can encourage China to join America and other Western nations in holding African partners accountable for their actions. Every effort must be made to convince them that it is in their best interest, as well, to participate in ensuring stability in the region.

Another way to shape perceptions of the United States is to take a hard look at the criticism of the United States militarizing diplomacy and make adjustments. Policy makers need to identify specific countries this may apply to and reevaluate how SFA is being conducted in that country. A way to reduce the U.S. footprint would be to develop a robust train-the-trainer program, where instead of inserting a cadre of trainers into an African country, a selected cadre of African trainers would be flown to the United States for training. Two things would happen. They would receive valuable training they can then pass on to their troops, and much like the International Military Education and Training (IMET) program they would be exposed to the U.S. values system and the American way of life. Since part of SC is gaining access, the United States could still maintain a small footprint in that country through other programs. At the same time, diplomacy and development efforts would need to be increased. This will happen naturally if the United States decides to rebalance its 3D approach.

Another way to dispel the notion that the United States has some nefarious military plot to take over the continent is to invest in establishing regional DoS headquarters complementary to the combatant commands. In looking at DoS' role in general regional engagement strategy, one author suggests establishing regional ambassadors who are "on par with the combatant commander with authority to synchronize, coordinate, and implement the regional engagement strategies."[55] He recommends a framework where "the regional ambassador would pull together all the various US military, civilian, and intelligence agencies involved in the region and report to the Secretary of State. Significant to this team is the inclusion of country ambassadors and the combatant commander as integral members.[56] He goes on to point out that the CGG would still report to and take orders from the Secretary of Defense in a wartime role and that the relationship he suggests between the GCC and regional ambassador is for steady-state activities. As the threat evolves, so must the United States, along with her allies and partners. In the 1980s, the United States realized it had to go joint. Today, it is imperative that we figure out how to work the interagency. In the 1980s, the United States prepared for a conventional fight. Today, we are faced with an asymmetrical threat that adapts to rapidly changing technologies and realities on the ground in places like the Maghreb and Sahel. We are faced with disenfranchised individuals and groups who will gravitate towards the option of joining terror organizations unless provided a suitable alternative option. The United States and the international community, through shaping efforts, must provide that suitable alternative option.

ENDNOTES:

[1] National Intelligence Council, *Global Trends 2015: A Dialogue about the Future with Nongovernment Experts* (Washington, DC: National Intelligence Council, 2000), 73.

[2] House Committee on Foreign Affairs, Africa and Global Health Subcommittee. *Africa Command: Opportunity for Enhanced Engagement or the Militarization of US-Africa Relations?: Testimony before the House Committee on Foreign Affairs, Subcommittee on Africa and Global Health.* 110th Cong., 1st sess., August 2, 2007, 48.

[3] Office of the President of the United States. *National Security Strategy 2010* (Washington, DC: Office of the President of the United States, 2010), 45.

[4] U.S. Department of Defense, *Joint Publication (JP) 3-0 Joint Operations* (Washington, DC: The Joint Staff, March 22, 2010), IV-27-28.

[5] Andrew C. McCarthy, "Fear the Muslim Brotherhood," *National Review Online*, January 31, 2011, http://www.nationalreview.com/articles/258419/fear-muslim-brotherhood-andrew-c-mccarthy.

[6] Lianne K. Boudali, *The GSPC: Newest Franchise in Al-Qa'ida's Global Jihad*, (West Point, NY: Combating Terrorism Center United States Military Academy, April, 2007), 1.

[7] Adam Nossiter, "Suicide Blast Wounds 2 at Embassy in Mauritania," *NY Times.com*, August 8, 2009, http://www.nytimes.com/2009/08/09/world/africa/09mauritania.html.

[8] Agence France-Presse, "Army attacks al Qaeda base, security forces say," Agence France-Presse, June 16, 2009, http://www.google.com/hostednews/afp/article/ALeqM5jlj0bwSTmJBEQDW3vG12t-6VGVeA.

[9] Jenny Booth, "Al-Qaeda kills British hostage Edwin Dyer, kidnapped in Mali after music festival," *Times Online*, June 3, 2009, http://www.timesonline.co.uk/tol/news/uk/article6420544.ece.

[10] Magharebia.com, "Kidnapped Mauritanian soldiers found beheaded; country seeks anti-terror help," *Magharebia.com*, September 21, 2008, http://www.magharebia.com/cocoon/awi/xhtml1/en_GB/features/awi/newsbriefs/general/2008/09/21/newsbrief-01.

[11] Lianne K. Boudali, *Examining US Counterterrorism Priorities and Strategy Across Africa's Sahel Region: Testimony Presented before the Senate Foreign Relations Committee, Subcomittee on African Affairs on November 17, 2009* (Santa Monica, CA: Rand, November 17, 2009), 2.

[12] Scott Johnson, "The Maghreb Myth," *Newsweek.com*, November 20, 2009, http://www.newsweek.com/2009/11/19/the-maghreb-myth.html.

[13] David Gutelius, *Examining US Counterterrorism Priorities and Strategy Across Africa's Sahel Region: Testimony Presented before the Senate Foreign Relations Committee, Subcomittee on African Affairs on November 17, 2009*, Senate Foreign Relations Committee Website, November 17, 2009, 5 http://foreign.senate.gov/imo/media/doc/GuteliusTestimony091117a1.pdf.

[14] Ann Hershkowitz, "The Tuareg and Mali and Niger: The Role of Desertification in Violent Conflict," *ICE Case Studies Number 151*, August, 2005 http://www.american.edu/ted/ice/tuareg.htm.

[15] Associated Press, "Gunmen fire on U.S. military plane in Mali," *USA Today.com*, September 13, 2007, http://www.usatoday.com/news/world/2007-09-13-us-mali_N.htm.

[16] Liana S. Wyler and Nicolas Cook, *Illegal Drug Trade in Africa: Trends and US policy*, CRS Report for Congress R40838 (Washington, DC: Congressional Research Service, February 26, 2010), 2.

[17] Ibid., 23.

[18] Will Ross, "History of crisis haunts Guinea-Bissau," *BBC News*, March 2, 2009, http://news.bbc.co.uk/2/hi/africa/7920033.stm.

[19] Liana S. Wyler and Nicolas Cook, *Illegal Drug Trade in Africa: Trends and US policy*, CRS Report for Congress R40838 (Washington, DC: Congressional Research Service, February 26, 2010), 5.

[20] Yahia H. Zoubir, "The United States and Maghreb–Sahel Security," *International Affairs 85: 5* (September 2009): 990-991.

[21] Stephanie Hanson, "China, Africa, and Oil," *Washington Post.com*, June 9, 2008, http://www.washingtonpost.com/wp-dyn/content/article/2008/06/09/AR2008060900714.html.

[22] Lauren Ploch, *Africa Command: US Strategic Interests and the Role of the US Military in Africa* CRS Report for Congress RL34003 (Washington, DC: Congressional Research Service, April 3, 2010), 4.

[23] Ibid., 5.

[24] Ibid., 8.

[25] Ibid., 26-27.

[26] Ibid., 8.

[27] USAID Website, http://www.usaid.gov/locations/sub-saharan_africa/.

[28] Catherine Dale and others, *The Department of Defense Role in Foreign Assistance: Background, Major Issues, and Options for Congress*, CRS Report for Congress RL34639 (Washington, DC: Congressional Research Service, August 25, 2008), 70.

[29] USAID Website. http://www.usaid.gov/locations/sub-saharan_africa/countries/warp/index.html.

[30] Dan Epstein (Bureau of African Affairs, U.S. Department of State), telephone conversation with author, March 17, 2011.

[31] Janet S. Morrison and Kathleen Hicks, *Integrating 21st Century Development and Security Assistance. Final Report of the Task Force on Non-Traditional Security Assistance, Center for Strategic and International Studies* (Washington, DC: Center for Strategic and International Studies Press, January 2008), 6.

[32] Catherine Dale and others, *The Department of Defense Role in Foreign Assistance: Background, Major Issues, and Options for Congress*, CRS Report for Congress RL34639 (Washington, DC: Congressional Research Service, August 25, 2008), 30-31.

[33] Dana Priest, *The Mission: Waging War and Keeping Peace with America's Military* (New York: W.W. Norton & Company, Inc., 2004), 14.

[34] Yahia H. Zoubir, "The United States and Maghreb–Sahel Security," *International Affairs 85: 5* (September 2009): 994.

[35] Senate Armed Services Committee & House Armed Services Committee. *William E. Ward's 2010 Posture Statement United States Africa Command,* 111th Cong., 2nd sess., March 9, 2010, 25.

[36] David Gutelius, *Examining US Counterterrorism Priorities and Strategy Across Africa's Sahel Region: Testimony Presented before the Senate Foreign Relations Committee, Subcomittee on African Affairs on November* 17, 2009, Senate Foreign Relations Committee Website, November 17, 2009, 2 http://foreign.senate.gov/imo/media/doc/GuteliusTestimony091117a1.pdf.

[37] Ibid., 2.

[38] Dan Epstein (Bureau of African Affairs, U.S. Department of State), telephone conversation with author, March 17, 2011.

[39] Office of the President of the United States. *National Security Presidential Directive/NSPD-44* (Washington, DC: Office of the President of the United States, December 7, 2005), 1.

[40] Harry R. Yarger, ed., Army War College . Strategic Studies Institute, and Army War College, 2010. *Short of General War : Perspectives on the Use of Military Power in the 21st Century.* Carlisle Papers. Carlisle, PA: Strategic Studies Institute, U.S. Army War College, https://www.strategicstudiesinstitute.army.mil/pdffiles/PUB983.pdf, 45.

[41] Clarence J. Bouchat, *An Introduction to Theater Strategy and Regional Security* (Carlisle, PA: Strategic Studies Institute, US Army War College, August 2007), 6.

[42] Harry R. Yarger, ed., Army War College . Strategic Studies Institute, and Army War College, 2010. *Short of General War : Perspectives on the Use of Military Power in the 21st Century.* Carlisle Papers. Carlisle, PA: Strategic Studies Institute, U.S. Army War College, https://www.strategicstudiesinstitute.army.mil/pdffiles/PUB983.pdf, 116.

[43] Dan Epstein (Bureau of African Affairs, U.S. Department of State), telephone conversation with author, March 17, 2011.

[44] Department of State, *Executive Budget Summary: Function 150 & Other International Programs, Fiscal Year 2012,* (Washington, DC: Department of State, February 14, 2011), 22 http://www.state.gov/documents/organization/156214.pdf.

[45] Ibid., 7.

[46] Harry R. Yarger, ed., Army War College . Strategic Studies Institute, and Army War College, 2010. *Short of General War : Perspectives on the Use of Military Power in the 21st Century.* Carlisle Papers. Carlisle, PA: Strategic Studies Institute, U.S. Army War College, https://www.strategicstudiesinstitute.army.mil/pdffiles/PUB983.pdf, 48-49.

[47] Michael Hughes, "Ambassador Blasts U.S. Militarization of Foreign Policy and Development" *Huffington Post*, February 18, 2011, http://www.huffingtonpost.com/michael-hughes/ambassador-blasts-us-mili_b_824938.html.

[48] Office of the President of the United States. *National Security Strategy 2002* (Washington, DC: Office of the President of the United States, 2002), 2-4.

[49] U.S. Department of the Army and Headquarters U.S. Marine Corps, *Counterinsurgency*, FM3-24 or MCWP 3-33.5 (Washington, DC: U.S. Department of the Army, December 2006), 6-3.

[50] David J. Kilcullen, "New Paradigms for 21st Century Conflict" *EJournal USA* 12 (5). [May 6, 2007], 42 http://www.america.gov/st/peacesec-english/2007/May/20080522172835SrenoD0.8730585.html.

[51] U.S. Department of State, *2010 Quadrennial Diplomacy and Development: Leading Through Civilian Power* (Washington, DC: Department of State, December 2010).

[52] James T. Conway, *Send in the Marines: A Marine Corps Operations Concept To Meet an Uncertain Security Environment* (January 2008), 16-23.

[53] Scott W. Power, "Security Force Assistance: An Enduring US Army Structure," (master's thesis, U.S. Army War College, 2010), 15, http://www.dtic.mil/cgi-bin/GetTRDoc?Location=U2&doc=GetTRDoc.pdf&AD=ADA522340.

[54] John A. Nagl, "Institutionalizing Adaptation: It's Time for a Permanent Army Advisor Corps," Center for a New American Strategy, June 27, 2007, 6.

[55] John S. Fant, "Diplomatic Leads: Strengthening the Role of the Department of State in US Regional Engagement Strategy," (Senior Service College Fellowship Project, U.S. Army War College, 2008), 15, http://www.dtic.mil/cgi-bin/GetTRDoc?Location=U2&doc=GetTRDoc.pdf&AD=ADA493714.

[56] Ibid., 18-19.

BIBLIOGRAPHY:

National Intelligence Council. *Global Trends 2015: A Dialogue about the Future with Nongovernment Experts.* Washington. DC: National Intelligence Council, 2000.

U.S. Congress. House. Committee on Foreign Affairs. Africa and Global Health Subcommittee. *Africa Command: Opportunity for Enhanced Engagement or the Militarization of US-Africa Relations?: Testimony before the House Committee on Foreign Affairs, Subcommittee on Africa and Global Health.* 110th Cong., 1st sess., August 2, 2007.

Office of the President of the United States. *National Security Strategy 2010.* Washington, DC: Office of the President of the United States, 2010.

U.S. Department of Defense. *Joint Publication (JP) 3-0 Joint Operations.* Washington, DC: The Joint Staff, March 22, 2010.

McCarthy, Andrew C. "Fear the Muslim Brotherhood." *National Review Online*, January 31, 2011, http://www.nationalreview.com/articles/258419/fear-muslim-brotherhood-andrew-c-mccarthy (accessed March 16, 2011).

Boudali, Lianne K. *The GSPC: Newest Franchise in Al-Qa'ida's Global Jihad.* West Point, NY: Combating Terrorism Center United States Military Academy, April, 2007.

Nossiter, Adam. "Suicide Blast Wounds 2 at Embassy in Mauritania." *NY Times.com,* August 8, 2009, http://www.nytimes.com/2009/08/09/world/africa/09mauritania.html (accessed March 16, 2011).

Agence France-Presse. "Army attacks al Qaeda base, security forces say." Agence France-Presse, June 16, 2009, http://www.google.com/hostednews/afp/article/ALeqM5jlj0bwSTmJBEQDW3vG12t-6VGVeA (accessed March 16, 2011).

Booth, Jenny. "Al-Qaeda kills British hostage Edwin Dyer, kidnapped in Mali after music festival." *Times Online*, June 3, 2009, http://www.timesonline.co.uk/tol/news/uk/article6420544.ece (accessed March 16, 2011).

Magharebia.com. "Kidnapped Mauritanian soldiers found beheaded; country seeks anti-terror help." *Magharebia.com*, September 21, 2008, http://www.magharebia.com/cocoon/awi/xhtml1/en_GB/features/awi/newsbriefs/general/2008/09/21/newsbrief-01 (accessed March 16, 2011).

Boudali, Lianne K. *Examining US Counterterrorism Priorities and Strategy Across Africa's Sahel Region: Testimony Presented before the Senate Foreign Relations Committee, Subcomittee on African Affairs on November 17, 2009.* Santa Monica, CA: Rand, November 17, 2009.

Johnson, Scott. "The Maghreb Myth." *Newsweek.com*, November 20, 2009, http://www.newsweek.com/2009/11/19/the-maghreb-myth.html (accessed February 15, 2011).

Gutelius, David. *"Examining US Counterterrorism Priorities and Strategy Across Africa's Sahel Region: Testimony Presented before the Senate Foreign Relations Committee, Subcomittee on African Affairs on November* 17, 2009," Senate Foreign Relations Committee Website, November 17, 2009, http://foreign.senate.gov/imo/media/doc/GuteliusTestimony091117a1.pdf (accessed March 17, 2011).

Hershkowitz, Ann. "The Tuareg and Mali and Niger: The Role of Desertification in Violent Conflict." *ICE Case Studies Number 151*, August, 2005 http://www.american.edu/ted/ice/tuareg.htm (accessed March 17, 2011).

Associated Press. "Gunmen fire on U.S. military plane in Mali." *USA Today.com*, September 13, 2007, http://www.usatoday.com/news/world/2007-09-13-us-mali_N.htm (accessed March 16, 2011).

Wyler, Liana S. and Nicolas Cook. *Illegal Drug Trade in Africa: Trends and US policy.* CRS Report for Congress R40838. Washington, DC: Congressional Research Service, February 26, 2010).

Ross, Will. "History of crisis haunts Guinea-Bissau." *BBC News*, March 2, 2009, http://news.bbc.co.uk/2/hi/africa/7920033.stm (accessed March 17, 2011).

Zoubir, Yahia H. "The United States and Maghreb–Sahel Security." *International Affairs 85: 5* (September 2009): 990-991.

Hanson, Stephanie. "China, Africa, and Oil." *Washington Post.com*, June 9, 2008, http://www.washingtonpost.com/wp-dyn/content/article/2008/06/09/AR2008060900714.html (accessed March 18, 2011).

Ploch, Lauren. *Africa Command: US Strategic Interests and the Role of the US Military in Africa.* CRS Report for Congress RL34003. Washington, DC: Congressional Research Service, April 3, 2010.

USAID Website, http://www.usaid.gov/locations/sub-saharan_africa/ (accessed March 19, 2011).

Dale, Catherine, Richard F. Grimmett, Rhoda Margesson, John Rollins, Tiaji Salaam-Blyther, Curt Tarnof, Amy F. Wolf, Liana Sun Wyler, and Steve Bowman. *The Department of Defense Role in Foreign Assistance: Background, Major Issues, and Options for Congress.* CRS Report for Congress RL34639. Washington, DC: Congressional Research Service, August 25, 2008.

USAID Website. http://www.usaid.gov/locations/sub-saharan_africa/countries/warp/index.html (accessed March 19, 2011).

Morrison, Janet S. and Kathleen Hicks. *Integrating 21st Century Development and Security Assistance. Final Report of the Task Force on Non-Traditional Security Assistance, Center for Strategic and International Studies.* Washington, DC: Center for Strategic and International Studies Press, January 2008.

Priest, Dana. *The Mission: Waging War and Keeping Peace with America's Military.* New York: W.W. Norton & Company, Inc., 2004.

U.S. Congress. House & Senate. Committees on Armed Services. *William E. Ward's 2010 Posture Statement United States Africa Command,* 111th Cong., 2nd sess., March 9, 2010.

Office of the President of the United States. *National Security Presidential Directive/NSPD-44.* Washington, DC: Office of the President of the United States, December 7, 2005.

Yarger, Harry R. ed., Army War College . Strategic Studies Institute, and Army War College, 2010. *"Short of General War : Perspectives on the Use of Military Power in the 21st Century."* Carlisle Papers. Carlisle, PA: Strategic Studies Institute, U.S. Army War College, https://www.strategicstudiesinstitute.army.mil/pdffiles/PUB983.pdf (accessed December 28, 2011).

Bouchat, Clarence J. *"An Introduction to Theater Strategy and Regional Security."* Carlisle, PA: Strategic Studies Institute, US Army War College, August 2007.

Department of State. *Executive Budget Summary: Function 150 & Other International Programs, Fiscal Year 2012.* Washington, DC: Department of State, February 14, 2011. http://www.state.gov/documents/organization/156214.pdf.

Hughes, Michael. "Ambassador Blasts U.S. Militarization of Foreign Policy and Development." *Huffington Post,* February 18, 2011, http://www.huffingtonpost.com/michael-hughes/ambassador-blasts-us-mili_b_824938.html (accessed March 19, 2011).

Office of the President of the United States. *National Security Strategy 2002.* Washington, DC: Office of the President of the United States, 2002.

U.S. Department of the Army, and Headquarters U.S. Marine Corps. *Counterinsurgency.* FM 3-24 or MCWP 3-33.5. Washington, DC: U.S. Department of the Army, December 2006.

Kilcullen, David J. "New Paradigms for 21st Century Conflict." *EJournal USA* 12 (5). (May 6, 2007). http://www.america.gov/st/peacesec-english/2007/May/20080522172835SrenoD0.8730585.html (accessed March 18, 2011

U.S. Department of State. *2010 Quadrennial Diplomacy and Development: Leading Through Civilian Power.* Washington, DC: Department of State, December 2010

Conway, James T. *Send in the Marines: A Marine Corps Operations Concept To Meet an Uncertain Security Environment.* January, 2008).

Power, Scott W. "Security Force Assistance: An Enduring US Army Structure." Masters Thesis, U.S. Army War College, 2010. http://www.dtic.mil/cgi-bin/GetTRDoc?Location=U2&doc=GetTRDoc.pdf&AD=ADA522340.

Nagl, John A. "Institutionalizing Adaptation: It's Time for a Permanent Army Advisor Corps." Center for a New American Strategy, June 27, 2007.

Fant, John S. "Diplomatic Leads: Strengthening the Role of the Department of State in US Regional Engagement Strategy." Senior Service College Fellowship Project, U.S. Army War College, 2008. http://www.dtic.mil/cgi-bin/GetTRDoc?Location=U2&doc=GetTRDoc.pdf&AD=ADA493714 (accessed March 18, 2011).

www.ingramcontent.com/pod-product-compliance
Lightning Source LLC
Chambersburg PA
CBHW080737290526
45790CB00008B/3232